Art in the Nineteenth Century

JILLIAN POWELL

Thomson Learning
New York

ART AND ARTISTS

Ancient Art
Art in the Nineteenth Century
Impressionism
Modern Art
Renaissance Art
Western Art 1600-1800

Cover *The Awakening Conscience* by William Holman Hunt. *Tate Gallery, London.*

Title page *The Gleaners* by Jean-François Millet. *Musée d'Orsay, Paris.*

First published in the
United States in 1995 by
Thomson Learning
115 Fifth Avenue
New York, NY 10003

First published in Great Britain in 1994 by
Wayland (Publishers) Limited

Library of Congress Cataloging-in-Publication Data
Powell, Jillian.
  Art in the nineteenth century / Jillian Powell.
      p.   cm.—(Art and artists)
  Includes bibliographical references and index.
  ISBN 1-56847-219-6
  1. Art, Modern—19th century—Juvenile literature.
[1. Art, Modern—19th century. 2. Art appreciation.]
I. Title. II. Series: Art and artists (Thomson Learning
(Firm))
N6450.P68   1995
709'.03'4—dc20   94-26769

Printed in Italy

Picture acknowledgments
The photographs in this book were supplied by: Archiv für Kunst und Geschichte 7, 12, 13 (left), 14, 15, 16, 18, 22, 26, 37, 41; Bridgeman Art Library main cover picture, ii, 4, 5, 8, 9 (left), 10, 13 (right), 17, 19 (both), 21, 23 (both), 24 (both), 25, 27 (both), 28, 29 (right), 30, 31, 32, 33, 34, 35, 38, 42 (both), 43, 44, 45, 46 (both); Christies Colour Library 29 (left); Hulton Deutsch Picture Library 9 (right), 11, 39 (right); Visual Arts Library cover, 20, 35, 39 (left); Wayland Picture Library/Tate Gallery 6-7,/British Museum 36, 40.

CONTENTS

1 INTRODUCTION

The nineteenth century was the beginning of the modern world. Wars and revolutions brought social and political change to Europe and America. Industrialization changed people's lives and the environment in which they lived and worked. Railroads and steamships allowed faster travel and expanded overseas trade. Telephone and telegraph systems opened up communications. The United States took on a new importance in international affairs, and European countries enlarged their empires by setting up colonies in other countries.

Manufacturing and trading middle classes became rich and powerful as industry boomed.

Left In his *Portrait of Madame Moitessier*, the French painter Jean-Auguste-Dominique Ingres (1780-1867) has shown her in splendid dress and jewelry, seated in a luxurious drawing room. Her pose, borrowed from classical art, gives her the grandeur of a goddess. *National Gallery, London.*

Above In the nineteenth century, landscape was a popular subject for painters in Europe and North America. Nature provided an escape from modern industrial life. Paintings such as *Twilight in the Wilderness*, by the American artist Frederick Edwin Church (1826-1900), could inspire a sense of wonder and spirituality. *Cleveland Museum of Art, Ohio.*

These middle classes began to take a new interest in their homes and in public buildings, such as town halls, factories, warehouses, and train stations. There was a steady demand for new buildings and for sculpture and paintings to decorate them. In earlier times, artists had relied on the Church or the State for patronage. Now, they had to compete for patrons by exhibiting their works in public shows and galleries.

Architects also entered their building designs in public competitions. This inspired a variety of new styles: Neoclassicism, Romanticism, Realism, and Impressionism all developed in the nineteenth century.

Derby Day by the English painter William Frith (1819-1909). Frith used the modern art of photography to provide many of the details for his panoramic view of the famous race meeting. *Tate Gallery, London.*

While the Industrial Revolution brought wealth to some, there was a growing awareness throughout the century of social discontent and poverty, especially in the crowded cities of Europe and North America. Nineteenth-century art and literature often reflected a desire to escape from the modern age, whether in nature, in a romanticized past – usually the Middle Ages – or in faraway places like North Africa.

People were attracted to life and art of the Middle Ages because they longed for the certainties of a lost age of faith. In 1859, Charles Darwin's *On the Origin of Species*

Beata Beatrix by the Pre-Raphaelite artist Dante Gabriel Rossetti (1828-1882). The English painter made this picture as a memorial to his wife, Elizabeth Siddal, who died in 1862. The painting represents the death of Beatrice, loved by the thirteenth-century Italian writer Dante. It shows a bird, a messenger of death, dropping the poppy of sleep into Beatrice's hands.
Tate Gallery, London.

challenged the creation story as told in the Bible, weakening religious faith and creating a mood of doubt and uncertainty. Artists were also facing new challenges. Photography meant that it was possible to record accurate images, thus questioning the very nature of the artist's role.

Photography and cheaper methods of printing, such as wood engraving and lithography, made reproductions of artwork available to a much wider audience. These new media also spread knowledge of foreign countries, archaeological discoveries, and the art of previous centuries, encouraging an interest in artistic styles of the

The Winnowers by the French Realist artist Gustave Courbet (1819-1877). He was one of the first artists to paint ordinary working people. *Musée des Beaux-Arts, Nantes, France.*

past. Artists responded to the challenge of photography in different ways. The Pre-Raphaelites in England, the French painter Eugène Delacroix, and the American artist Thomas Eakins all used photographs to help them with their painting. The Victorian artist William Frith, popular as a "genre" artist (painting everyday activities), used several photographs of the grandstand crowds on Derby Day to compose his famous scene at the races (see page 6). Some painters tried to make their paintings look like photographs, using minutely detailed brushwork and a smooth finish. Others reacted against the photographic image, believing the artist should create his or her own image. Free brushwork, swirling paint, and the dominance of color, tone, and pattern over line meant that by the end of the century the Impressionists and artists like James Abbott McNeill Whistler (see also pages 44-45) and Philip Wilson Steer were heralding a new age of abstract art.

The interior of Joseph Paxton's Crystal Palace. It was opened in London's Hyde Park by Queen Victoria for the Great Exhibition in 1851.

Arrangement in Gray and Black, No. 1: The Artist's Mother, by James Abbott McNeill Whistler (1834-1903). Whistler's streamlined composition and strong sense of shape and pattern anticipate art of the following century. *Musée d'Orsay, Paris.*

In architecture, the mass production of new materials such as cast iron and steel and the demand for different kinds of buildings created new possibilities for architects and engineers. Iron and steel were used to span the vast spaces needed for train stations and other large buildings with high ceilings.

The Crystal Palace, built entirely from cast iron and glass in London's Hyde Park, was designed by Sir Joseph Paxton to house the Great Exhibition of 1851. The Eiffel Tower, in Paris, was constructed in steel by Alexandre-Gustave Eiffel in 1889. Lack of space in cities, new materials, and the invention of the elevator encouraged high-rise building. As a result the first skyscrapers were built in New York City and Chicago by the end of the century. Historical styles of architecture (known as "Revivalist") were widely used for every kind of building, from grand Neoclassical museums and town halls to soaring Gothic Revival churches.

2 NEOCLASSICISM AND ROMANTICISM

This *Portrait of Madame Recamier* by Jacques-Louis David (1748-1825) is a perfect example of Neoclassical simplicity. *Musée du Louvre, Paris.*

During the eighteenth century, archaeological discoveries in Greece and Rome and a revival of the study of classical art and literature encouraged the development of a new artistic style: Neoclassicism. In France, the Neoclassical style became very fashionable during the French Revolution (1789-1799), when heroic, moral themes from classical history were chosen to inspire the revolutionary cause. The Neoclassical style is best represented by the works of the painter Jacques-Louis David and the sculptors Antonio Canova and Bertel Thorvaldsen (see chapter 6).

David's *Oath of the Horatii*, painted in 1785, illustrated the Neoclassical ideals of a serious, moral theme with simple composition and cool, plain colors. Sculptors also chose classical subjects, carving statues in calm poses inspired by Greek or Roman sculpture. They often used

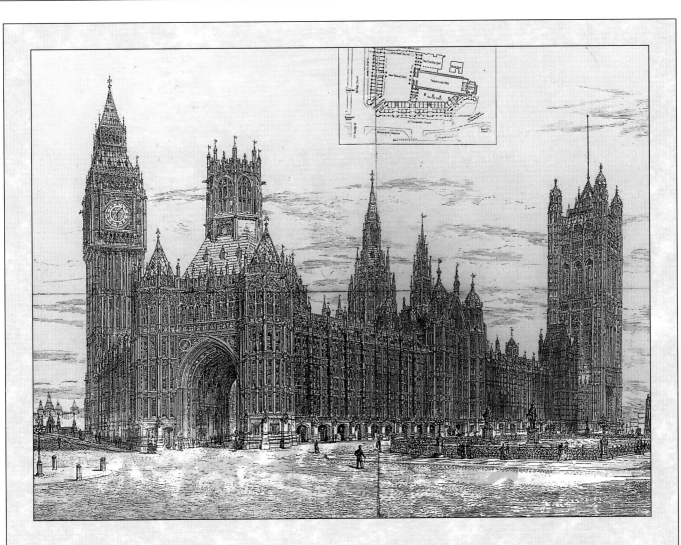

The Battle of the Styles
After the Houses of Parliament in London burned down in 1834, a competition was held to choose the design for the new building. Neoclassical designs competed with Gothic Revival design in a grand Battle of the Styles. In the end, the Gothic Revival design won and Sir Charles Barry (1795-1860) was appointed architect, with Augustus Pugin (1812-1852) responsible for the design of the detail and furnishings.

white Carrara marble, which was polished to a smooth finish.

By the early nineteenth century, the fashion for Neoclassicism was influencing architecture, furniture, ceramics, textiles, and clothing. Even hairstyles "in the Greek fashion" became popular. Artists continued to look to classical history and mythology for themes, but they also applied the Neoclassical style to subjects taken from the Bible and from poetry. Jean-Auguste Ingres, who was a pupil of David, painted portraits and nudes in the Neoclassical style as well as historical and literary subjects. He believed that line was much more important than color in a painting, and whatever their subject, his paintings have a quality of stillness and calm derived from the works of classical Greece and Rome (see page 5).

Soon a different mood was influencing literature and the visual arts. Neoclassicism was being challenged by new interests: the exotic and the faraway, the distant past (especially the romanticized Middle Ages), and the new importance attached to feelings and emotions. The calm, order, and sense of purpose that were features of the Neoclassical style were replaced by the drama, struggle, and emotion of Romanticism.

Artists in Europe and America began to explore new subjects. In France, Romanticism reflected the mood of melancholy and despair that followed defeat at the Battle of Waterloo in 1815, at the end of the Napoleonic Wars. Artists painted soldiers fleeing the battlefield, horses rearing in terror, and scenes of fear and destruction.

For his *Raft of the Medusa,* Théodore Géricault took a tragic and scandalous subject from the news. The *Medusa* was a government-owned ship that had sunk off the west coast of Africa. A few survivors floated for days on a raft and were driven to starvation, madness, and cannibalism. Géricault approached this modern news story as if it had a great historical theme, painting it on a huge canvas in somber colors with a dramatic, pyramid-shaped group of figures. The new interests of Romanticism were also shown in Géricault's portraits of patients in a mental asylum and in his melancholy lithographs of the streets of London, inspired by a trip to England in 1821.

Romantic themes were also provided by English writers including William Shakespeare and Lord George Gordon Byron and Scotsman

Left The dramatic painting *Raft of the Medusa*, by Théodore Géricault (1791-1824). *Musée d'Orsay, Paris.*

Above *Massacre at Chios,* a tragic episode recorded by Eugène Delacroix (1798-1863). *Musée du Louvre, Paris.*

Above *The Cross in the Mountains,* by Caspar David Friedrich (1774-1840), was commissioned as an altarpiece for a private chapel. *Staatliche Kunstsammlungen, Dresden, Germany.*

Sir Walter Scott. The *Death of Sardanapalus* by Eugène Delacroix was a violent scene taken from a poem by Byron of a cruel ruler who ordered all his slaves, mistresses, and horses put to death.

In Germany, Romanticism had begun to affect literature in the late eighteenth century. The works of writers like Johann Wolfgang von Goethe and Friedrich von Schiller stressed the importance of feeling, emotion, and romantic love and looked to the historical past and to nature for inspiration and spiritual comfort. In the nineteenth century, German painters took up these themes, using landscape to convey spiritual feeling. The paintings of Otto Philipp Runge (1777-1810) combine mystical feeling and religious symbolism with accurate scientific observation. He worked on a series of

paintings called *The Times of Day*, which he intended to be hung in a specially designed chapel where specially composed music would be played.

Caspar David Friedrich believed "a painter should paint not only what he sees before him but also what he sees within himself." His landscapes were usually lonely, remote places in the mountains or along the Baltic seashore, in the twilight of sunrise or sunset, or in moonlight. Solitary figures added to the mood of melancholy and loneliness. Friedrich's landscapes were full of symbolism: he used rocks to represent Christianity and winding paths to show the "path of life." A sense of stillness, created by the somber lighting and his precise brushwork, heightened the religious feeling in his landscapes.

While some artists looked to nature to provide spiritual comfort or inspiration, others looked to the historical past. "The Nazarenes," a group of young German painters working in Italy in the early years of the nineteenth century, aimed to revive the art of the Middle Ages, which they felt was true and direct in style and feeling. They founded a group called the Lucas Brotherhood, or Nazarenes, based on a medieval painters' guild, and lived as artist-monks in an abandoned monastery in Rome, growing their hair long, wearing medieval-style clothes, and painting, praying, and singing together. The leaders, Franz Pforr (1788-1812) and Friedrich Overbeck (1789-1869), met in 1808 when they were art students in Vienna. They rebelled against their academic training, which was based on classical Greek and Roman and High Renaissance art, and began to study fifteenth-century painters, including Dürer and Perugino, and the early works of Raphael. They copied the methods and styles

Left *Italia and Germania* by Friedrich Overbeck. The two women represent Italy and Germany. The Nazarene artists wanted to bring together the best of Italian and Northern European traditions of art. *Gemäldegalerie Neue Meister, Dresden, Germany.*

Above *The Wise and Foolish Virgins* by Peter von Cornelius (1783-1867) is based on the parable of the ten virgins in the New Testament of the Bible. *Gemälde, Düsseldorf, Germany.*

of these artists, sometimes working in the medium of tempera (colors mixed with egg yolk) rather than oils and learning the technique of fresco. They chose historical subjects, like Pforr's *Entry of the Emperor Rudolf into Basel, 1273*, which he painted in clear, bright colors and with careful, detailed brushwork.

Although Pforr died when he was only 24 years old, other artists joined the group and carried on his ideas. Peter von Cornelius aimed to revive the art of fresco and painted several large murals in churches and other public buildings in Munich.

Like other breakaway groups in the nineteenth century, the Nazarenes wanted to revive art by returning to the style and methods of the Middle Ages. Their fascination with medieval life and art is one of the constant themes of Romantic Art.

3 ENGLISH LANDSCAPE PAINTING

In the nineteenth century, people began to take much more interest in landscape painting, and this form of art became more highly valued by art critics. Previously, "view painting" had been considered a humble form of art, much less important than paintings of Biblical, classical, or historical themes. A new interest in landscape developed in England in the eighteenth century, with the fashion for visiting picturesque places and with the creation of landscaped parks and gardens by the landscape artist Lancelot "Capability" Brown (1715-1783) and his followers. Romantic writers such as the English Lake poets William Wordsworth and Samuel Taylor Coleridge and the French philosopher Jean-Jacques Rousseau encouraged the "back to nature" movement. They showed how the countryside could offer escape and peace in the modern industrial world.

Left *Flatford Mill* by John Constable (1776-1837). This painting is typical of Constable's large oil landscapes. It shows a tranquil summer scene beside the Stour River in Suffolk, England. *Tate Gallery, London.*

Above Constable's *Branch Hill Pond, Hampstead.* The artist painted many light oil sketches like this one, as well as huge finished works such as *Flatford Mill,* opposite. *Victoria and Albert Museum, London.*

Some English artists followed the Dutch landscape masters of the seventeenth century in painting their own local countrysides. John Constable painted landscapes of the Stour River valley in Suffolk, England, where he was born. His paintings were usually set in spring or high summer, with the trees in full leaf, and showed simple scenes like a horse being ferried across the river or a man opening the lock gates. Even after he had moved to

London, Constable continued to paint the Suffolk landscape he loved so much. He once wrote, "The sound of water escaping from mill dams, etc., willows, old rotten planks, slimy posts and brickwork – I love such things. Painting with me is but another word for feeling."

Constable believed artists should work directly from nature, and he made lots of sketches in

pencil, watercolor, and oil, which he used to compose his large landscapes in the studio. He made a special study of clouds and weather, believing that the sky was the most important element in a landscape. He was always trying new methods of capturing the freshness and bloom of nature – the effect of sunlight after rain or wind in the leaves or on water. But his experiments – such as scattered highlights of white – were often attacked by the critics, and his landscapes were repeatedly rejected by the Royal Academy for being too humble in their subject matter or "too green."

While Constable concentrated on local scenery, his rival at the Royal Academy, Joseph Mallord William Turner, looked more widely for inspiration: to Italy, to the Bible and literature, and to the seventeenth-century masters of

The Norwich School
In choosing to paint local scenery, John Constable was following the example of seventeenth-century Dutch landscape artists such as Jacob van Ruisdael and Meindert Hobbema. Other nineteenth-century painters also painted local scenery, grouping into regional schools and concentrating on one area of countryside. They include the Barbizon painters in France (see pages 33 and 34) and the Norwich School in England. The artists of the Norwich School (in Norfolk), led by John Crome (1768-1821) and John Sell Cotman (1782-1842), held exhibitions of their paintings at a house in Norwich between 1805 and 1825. They painted the wide, flat landscape and open skies of Norfolk in fresh oils and watercolors.

Left *Heaving Coals by Moonlight* by J. M. W. Turner (1775-1851). Here Turner has painted the shapes of ships' hulls and rigging dissolving in silvery moonlight. *National Gallery of Art, Washington D.C.*

Above *Landscape Scene in Norfolk* by John Crome. Crome's picturesque scenery and somber, warm coloring shows the influence of seventeenth-century Dutch artists. *Bury Art Gallery and Museum, Bury, England.*

French classical landscape painting, Claude Lorraine and Nicolas Poussin. Turner began his career painting watercolors of buildings and places, but he soon became interested in recording the changing effects of atmosphere, light, and weather. He sketched landscapes in oil and watercolor, using his sketches and memory to compose large, finished works in the studio. *Snowstorm: Hannibal and his Army Crossing the Alps* took a story from classical history combined with Turner's experience of a violent storm in Yorkshire. Some of his landscapes, although painted from the English countryside, were composed in the manner of Claude and Poussin. Turner wanted landscape art to be more highly regarded, and he worked on a series of landscapes for engraving in a book he called the *Liber Studiorum* (Book of Studies). He had favorite

Samuel Palmer

In the nineteenth century, landscape art was used by painters to convey mood and feelings. This was particularly true with the works of Samuel Palmer (1805-1881). Palmer was born in London and began showing his landscape drawings at the Royal Academy at the age of fourteen. He settled in the village of Shoreham in Kent, where he joined a group of artists who called themselves "The Ancients." They included John Linnell (1792-1882), Edward Calvert (1799-1883), and George Richmond (1809-1896). Like the Nazarenes (see pages 14 and 15), The Ancients lived simple lives, concentrating on their art. Palmer painted small, jewel-like landscapes in watercolor or sepia ink, and his works have an intense, spiritual feeling. Throughout his life he was greatly influenced by the visionary artist-poet William Blake (see page 38). With *In a Shoreham Garden* (above), Palmer conveys the exuberance of nature. *Victoria and Albert Museum, London.*

Burning of the Houses of Parliament. Turner recorded this dramatic episode in 1834. The fire provided him with an exciting subject, with flames and smoke reflected in the Thames River. *Philadelphia Museum of Art.*

themes he returned to time and again: the sea, dramatic storms, sunrise, and sunset.

In 1819 Turner made the first of several visits to Italy, where the brilliant light and sunshine inspired him to experiment with new ways of representing light and atmosphere. His compositions became freer and more abstract, sometimes based on a swirling, circular shape. He loved the effects of steam, smoke, or mist, dissolving form into pure color, as in *Burning of the Houses of Parliament* or *Rain Steam, and Speed – The Great Western Railway*. Critics thought his later works looked strange with their shimmering veils of color, and called them "pictures of nothing, and very like." They were amazed that Turner often completed his pictures as they hung on the walls of the Royal Academy just before an exhibition opened. In his exhibition works and in his spontaneous sketches, which he called "color beginnings," Turner brought a new approach to landscape art.

Thomas Girtin
Another English painter, Thomas Girtin (1775-1802), worked closely with Turner in the mid-1790s. Girtin painted with watercolors and was the first artist to realize the possibilities of this medium. He was only 27 when he died, but during his short life he revolutionized landscape painting in watercolors, at which he excelled.

4 ART IN NORTH AMERICA

Home in the Woods by Thomas Cole (1801-1848). In this painting Cole depicts the struggle of early American settlers to survive in a wild, untamed countryside. *Reynolds Museum, Winston-Salem, North Carolina.*

In the early nineteenth century, much of the American continent was still wild, unspoiled country. But there was already awareness that this natural paradise could be threatened by advancing civilization. The artist Thomas Cole wrote, "The painter of American scenery has, indeed, privileges superior to any other; all nature here is new to art."

Cole was the first American painter to concentrate on landscapes. He traveled from New York City along the Hudson River Valley in search of scenery, founding the first school of American painting, the Hudson River School. Cole's landscapes are often breathtaking panoramas, with human figures dwarfed by wild countryside stretching away to a wide horizon. He also painted landscapes with historical or allegorical themes, such as the decline and fall of civilizations, or "the voyage of life."

Asher B. Durand (1796-1886), another painter in the Hudson River School, liked to paint outside. His views of the Hudson Valley showed careful detail that reflected his training as an engraver. Cole's pupil Frederick Church (1826-1900) traveled farther afield to South America, the Alps, and the Arctic in search of the awe-inspiring scenery of mountains, jungles, and rocky deserts (see picture on page 5). His subjects included Niagara Falls, the icebergs of the Arctic, and the volcanic mountain of Cotopaxi in Ecuador.

Sunset Going Down Over the Sea by the luminist painter John Frederick Kensett. The painter has concentrated entirely on the light of sunset, reducing his composition to sea and sky only. *Metropolitan Museum of Art, New York.*

By the middle of the century, painters including John Frederick Kensett (1816-1872), Fitz Hugh Lane (1804-1865), and Martin Johnson Heade (1819-1904) were showing increasing interest in capturing the effects of light and atmosphere. These effects have come to be known as luminism, a word used to describe landscapes painted in a brilliant midday light, with every detail in telescopic focus and an almost magical stillness. In a luminist landscape, there is an overwhelming sense of light, space, and air.

Folk or primitive art became very popular in North America in the nineteenth century. Folk artists usually had no professional training and often worked anonymously, selling their paintings as they traveled from place to place. Portraits, landscapes, and pictures of farm and wild animals were all popular subjects.

The best known of the American primitive artists of the early nineteenth century is Edward Hicks (1780-1849), who began his career as a coach and sign painter. He was a Quaker and he painted many pictures with Biblical themes. There are over a hundred versions of his *Peacable Kingdom,* which takes its theme from a Bible story about people and animals all living in harmony together.

Fur Trappers Descending the Missouri by George Caleb Bingham. Bingham's painting captures the stillness and tranquillity of the river. *Metropolitan Museum of Art, New York.*

Genre painting, showing everyday life and activities, was inspired by the wild and sometimes dangerous lives of the European pioneers and the Native Americans. It became popular in America in the early nineteenth century. Paintings by artists like George Caleb Bingham (1811-1879) and George Catlin (1796-1872) captured the sense of adventure in a land where nature was still untamed. Bingham painted in the frontier areas of Missouri and the Midwest, recording the lives of boatmen, fur trappers, and settlers along the Missouri River. There is a haunting silence and stillness about his river scenes, which are full of light, air, and reflections. William Sidney Mount

North American wildlife

Some of the plant and animal life of the North American countryside was captured in the beautiful watercolors of John James Audubon (1785-1851). Audubon was born in the West Indies and brought up in France, where he became interested in drawing birds and other subjects from nature. He settled in North America in 1803, painting portraits and teaching drawing to earn a living. He followed his special interests of hunting, painting wildlife, and taxidermy (the process of stuffing animal skins) in his spare time. By the 1820s he was working on his masterpiece, the illustrations for *Birds of America,* which recorded almost five hundred native species in watercolor drawings. (See his *Ivory-billed Woodpecker,* above.)

The Blue Boat by Winslow Homer. Homer painted this watercolor in a crisp, fresh style that shows the influence of Japanese prints. *Private collection.*

The Gross Clinic by Thomas Eakins. With this subject Eakins was following a tradition that included artists like the great seventeenth-century Dutch painter Rembrandt. *Jefferson College, Philadelphia.*

(1807-1868) painted life on Long Island, New York, where he was born. He followed the Dutch genre painters of the seventeenth century, choosing scenes of work and leisure in domestic or rural settings – cider-making, bargaining for a horse, mending tools, or dancing. Catlin and Seth Eastman (1808-1875) recorded with accuracy and detail the lives and customs of the Native Americans, who were fast disappearing with the advance of the white settlers.

Winslow Homer (1836-1910) trained as a lithographer and began his career engraving scenes from the Civil War (1861-1865) for the magazine *Harper's Weekly*. His later genre paintings ranged from simple domestic or rural scenes, such as berry picking in the autumn or a country classroom, to life in the fashionable seaside resorts. With his careful observation of light and weather and his fresh, unsentimental approach, Homer brought a new realism to American genre painting.

Thomas Eakins (1844-1916) trained in Paris in the 1860s, where he saw the work of the Realist painter Gustave Courbet (see pages 32 and 33) and studied earlier artists including the seventeenth-century Spanish artist Diego Velázquez. Back in America, Eakins developed his own Realist style, making careful, scientific studies of perspective, anatomy, and light and using the new art of photography to help him understand form and movement. He even dissected corpses while researching *The Gross Clinic*, which shows a surgeon working on a dissection in front of his students. The painting shocked the public and the art critics with its realistic treatment of the subject.

5 THE PRE-RAPHAELITES

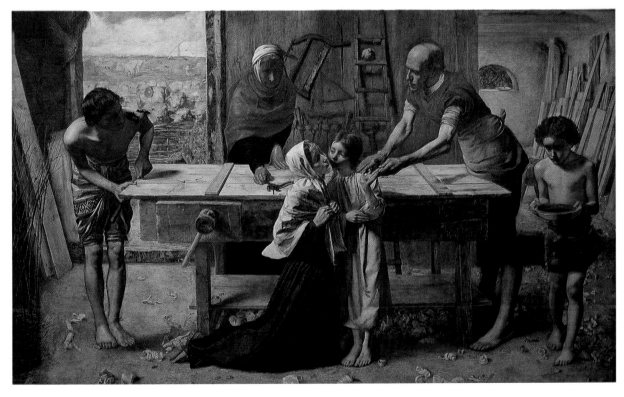

When first shown, John Millais's *Christ in the House of His Parents* was criticized for showing the holy family in a humble, realistic setting. *Tate Gallery, London.*

In 1848 a number of paintings shown at the Royal Academy in London were signed with the secret initials P.R.B. The Pre-Raphaelite Brotherhood was a group of young artists, all about 20 years old. They were rebelling against the style of art that was being taught at the Royal Academy and at other art schools, which they considered to be artificial in subject and style and dark and muddy in color. They looked back to artists of the fifteenth century – before the time of the Renaissance master Raphael – who inspired them with their serious subjects, careful, detailed brushwork, and bright, fresh colors.

The Pre-Raphaelites were led by John Everett Millais (1829-1896), William Holman Hunt (1827-1910), and Dante Gabriel Rossetti (1828-1882). They talked together, wrote down their

ideas on art, and made a list of all the artists and other famous people they admired. They chose subjects from the Bible or from poetry and legend, using sources from Shakespeare, the poets Keats and Tennyson, and the legend of King Arthur. They tried to paint their subjects as truthfully and accurately as possible, making careful studies of every detail, from medieval swords and spears to wild flowers and foliage. They used bright colors, painting on a wet, white background so that their paintings looked much lighter and fresher than others of the time, which were usually painted on a brown background.

Rossetti's painting of the Annunciation of the Virgin Mary, *Ecce Ancilla Domini* (see page 27), was painted in bright, primary colors with lots of white. Millais's *Christ in the House of*

Above Millais's *Ophelia*. Rossetti's wife, Elizabeth Siddal, posed for this painting of the tragic drowning scene from Shakespeare's *Hamlet. Tate Gallery, London.*

His Parents shocked the critics and the public because it showed Jesus as an ordinary boy with his family in a real, humble carpenter's shop. The novelist Charles Dickens attacked it as "mean, repulsive and revolting," but the influential critic John Ruskin came to the Pre-Raphaelites' defense.

The Pre-Raphaelites believed that art should have a serious, moral purpose. In addition to subjects from the Bible, they painted social themes, such as Hunt's *The Awakening Conscience* (see cover), which shows an unmarried woman realizing that she must give up her relationship with her lover. Set in a typical English Victorian sitting room, the picture is full of symbolism, such as the cat playing with a bird under the table and the print above the piano of the Biblical story of the woman who committed adultery.

Scenes from literature were also popular. For Millais's *Ophelia*, a tragic scene from Shakespeare's *Hamlet*, the favorite Pre-Raphaelite model Elizabeth Siddal posed in a bath kept warm by lamps placed underneath it.

Above *The Last of England* by Ford Madox Brown. This painting was inspired by the often sad departure of emigrants to the far-off shores of Australia. *Birmingham City Art Gallery.*

Left In his painting of the Annunciation, *Ecce Ancilla Domini*, Dante Gabriel Rossetti tried to portray a simple vision of the Virgin Mary, using lots of white to convey purity. *Tate Gallery, London.*

Mallais painted the background from nature on the banks of the Ewell River in Surrey. Rossetti's favorite writer was the Italian medieval poet Dante, and he made many small, jewel-like oil and watercolor paintings illustrating scenes from Dante's life and poetry.

The Pre-Raphaelite Brotherhood lasted less than ten years as a group, but other artists took up the Pre-Raphaelite style and subjects of painting. Ford Madox Brown (1821-1893) painted *Work* in 1865, showing a street scene near the artist's home in London. The painting depicted all the different social classes that made up Victorian society, from street beggars to the leisured upper classes. Even the dogs in the picture represented different social classes.

Brown's best known painting, *The Last of England*, showed emigrants on a ship leaving for Australia. He also painted landscapes in the Pre-Raphaelite style, as did William Holman Hunt and another very popular artist, William Dyce (1806-1864).

6 SCULPTURE IN THE NINETEENTH CENTURY

The Three Graces, by Antonio Canova. The sculptor has borrowed classical ideals to create a Neoclassical sculpture with beautiful flowing forms carved from smooth white Carrara marble. *Belvoir Castle, Leicestershire, England.*

Sculpture was a popular form of art during the nineteenth century. Bronze or stone statues commemorating heroes or important events were set up in public streets and squares. Today nineteenth century sculpture can still be seen in city centers, parks, churches, and graveyards. Sculpture was also widely used to decorate the inside and outside of town halls, opera houses, theaters, hotels, and private houses.

Like painters of the time, sculptors worked in a variety of styles, but Neoclassicism, inspired by the classical statues of Greece and Rome, was the dominant style. The outstanding Neoclassical sculptors of the early nineteenth century were the Italian Antonio Canova (1757-1822) and the Dane Bertel Thorvaldsen (1770-1844), who settled in Rome in 1797. Both men carved calm, idealized statues in smooth white Carrara marble, representing classical subjects or portraits of patrons in the Neoclassical style, like Thorvaldsen's portrait bust of the banker Thomas Hope or Canova's portrait of Pauline Borghese as a reclining Venus. One of the most popular statues of the century was the Neoclassical nude *Greek Slave* by the American sculptor Hiram Powers

Above *Stag Attacked by a Panther* by Antoine-Louis Barye. This animal group is typical of Barye's lively, often violent sculptures. *Christie's, London.*

Right *Greek Slave* sculpted by Hiram Powers. This statue became one of the most popular sculptures of the nineteenth century. *Private collection.*

(1805-1873). It was taken on tour in the United States in 1847 and was a great success when shown at the Great Exhibition in London in 1851. Replicas of the statue were sold to private collectors in Europe and the United States.

Romanticism did not have the same impact on sculpture as it had on painting. But it was reflected in the emotion and energy of works like *Departure of the Volunteers* by François Rude (1784-1855), which is carved on the Arc de Triomphe in Paris and inspired the crowded sculptures of Auguste Préault (1809-1879).

Antoine-Louis Barye (1795-1875) specialized in dramatic, often violent animal groups and figures. He had begun his career working for a goldsmith, making small animal figures for jewelry. In 1831 he cast his first large-scale bronze of a tiger. Barye worked from sketches of wild animals in the Paris Zoo, bringing his sculptures to life by their lively modeling and the flickering play of light over their surfaces.

The most celebrated sculptor of the nineteenth century was Auguste Rodin (1840-1917). He was born in Paris and studied drawing with the

Left *The Thinker*, one of the most celebrated works of Auguste Rodin. It was originally intended as one of the figures to decorate the gates for a proposed new museum in Paris. *Musée Rodin, Paris.*

Right Rodin's sculpture of Honoré de Balzac wrapped in a cloak that hides his body was rejected in 1893 as being too ugly. The statue was not erected until years later and is now in Place Brea-Vavin, Paris.

sculptor Barye. From about 1864 he worked as a mason, carving decorative figures for the Stock Exchange building in Brussels. In 1875 he visited Italy, where he studied classical and Renaissance sculpture, including the works of Michelangelo. Two years later, Rodin exhibited his first lifesize statue, *The Age of Bronze*, which was so lifelike that the artist was accused of making a plaster cast directly from the model! The figures that followed, the *Walking Man* and the study for *St. John the Baptist Preaching*, showed the same lifelike quality.

Rodin sketched live models in his studio before modeling his works in wax or clay. Casts might then be made from bronze, or marble carved following the wax or clay model. Rodin wanted to make sculptures that would be touched as well as seen, and he used expressive poses and broken, textured surfaces to create interest and convey emotion or energy. Some critics thought his works often looked sketchy or unfinished, similar to Impressionist paintings (see page 35), but for Rodin even part of a figure could be a complete sculpture.

In 1879, Rodin was commissioned to make the gates for a new museum of decorative arts in Paris. Rodin's gates, called *Gates of Hell,* were inspired by Ghiberti's *Gates of Paradise*, made for the baptistery of the cathedral in Florence in the fifteenth century. Ghiberti had worked in regular bronze panels, but Rodin's design was much freer, allowing his figures to twist and flow. In the end, the museum was never completed and neither were the gates, but the commission did give Rodin ideas for more than two hundred sculptures, including *The Thinker* (above left) and *The Kiss.*

Although Rodin became very famous, some of his works were strongly criticized. His sculpture of the novelist Honoré de Balzac (above) was attacked as formless and ugly and was rejected by the people who commissioned it. Today, Balzac is one of Rodin's most famous portraits of nineteenth-century celebrities, which included the writers Charles-Pierre Baudelaire and George Bernard Shaw, the composer Gustav Mahler, and the dancer Vaslav Nijinsky. After his death in 1917, the sculptor's last studio in Paris was opened as the Rodin Museum.

7 REALISM IN FRANCE

The Stone Breakers by Gustave Courbet. Courbet was an ardent socialist, whose paintings, showing everyday lives of hardship and poverty, conveyed a social message. *Staatliche Kunstsammlungen, Dresden, Germany.*

By the middle of the nineteenth century, there was growing awareness of the social and economic problems caused by the Industrial Revolution. There was widespread unemployment and poverty in the cities, and those who were lucky enough to have jobs often suffered long hours and poor working conditions. The concern of some artists and writers about these problems was reflected in their works, which showed the lives of ordinary people at work and at home. These artists were known as Realists.

Realist art often shocked both critics and the public because it broke the rules taught by art schools. Realist artists began painting humble, everyday subjects on a scale previously used only for grand Biblical,

historical, or classical subjects. They also experimented with new ways of handling paint, using broad brush strokes and thicker paint, so that the picture itself had texture and interest. Some artists used photographs to help them understand form and movement or to compose their pictures.

In France, the leading Realist painter was Gustave Courbet (1819-1877). He painted simple, everyday subjects like the country funeral *Burial at Ornans. The Stone Breakers* (above) shows two men hard at work, breaking stones by a roadside. Courbet used thick paint handled with a broad brush or a palette knife and drab, earthy colors. He said, "Painting is an essentially concrete art and can only consist of the presentation of real and existing things.

Above *The Water Gate*, a peaceful riverside scene by Charles-François Daubigny. Daubigny was one of the Barbizon painters, a group of artists who encouraged the practice of painting outdoors. *Musée d'Orsay, Paris.*

Right *Fields with Trees and Cottages* by Jean-Baptiste-Camille Corot. He produced a huge number of works and his later paintings have a dreamlike quality, with misty coloring and flickering light. *Christie's, London.*

I cannot paint an angel because I have never seen one." When Courbet painted nudes they were real people, not idealized figures, and when he painted landscapes or seascapes they were of real places. (See page 8.)

After his paintings were criticized for being vulgar and rejected by the International Exhibition in Paris in 1855, Courbet set up his own Realist exhibition. In his life, as well as in his art, he was a rebel. He was imprisoned for a while, then forced into exile in Switzerland after taking part in riots supporting the Paris Commune of 1871. This committee opposed the French government, and during that time crowds took to the streets to demonstrate the power of the ordinary people against the French National Assembly.

Realism dealt with modern, everyday subjects, showing the lives of ordinary people, but it also changed the way artists looked at the landscape. In France, the influence of the English Landscape School began to be felt from the 1820s with an exhibition of Constable's paintings in Paris and the works of English artists living in France, such as Richard Parkes Bonington (1801-1828). These artists encouraged sketching from nature, outdoors. Georges Michel (1763-1843) painted the fields and heaths around Paris with bold, free brushwork and dark earthy colors. Like Michel, Jean-Baptiste-Camille Corot (1796-1875) began sketching landscapes in oil in the open air, but the brilliant light of Italy, which he visited in 1824, encouraged him to mix white with all his colors, giving them a fresh, light quality.

The Gleaners by Jean-François Millet. This picture of poor women gathering scraps of wheat after the harvest became one of the best-known paintings of the nineteenth century. *Musée d'Orsay, Paris.*

In the 1830s, a group of landscape artists settled around the village of Barbizon in the Forest of Fontainebleau near Paris. The Barbizon painters included Théodore Rousseau (1812-1867) and Charles François Daubigny (1817-1878). They wanted to leave city life behind and paint directly from nature in the open air. Rousseau was especially interested in effects of weather and light at different times of day. Daubigny painted peaceful river scenes from his studio boat on the Seine and Oise rivers. In their desire to paint in the open air and to capture subtle changes in light and weather, the Barbizon School anticipated the work of the Impressionists (see opposite page).

Jean-François Millet (1814-1875) knew and worked alongside the painters at Barbizon, where he settled in 1849, living in great poverty. Millet concentrated on painting simple rural landscapes, showing peasants working in the fields. Paintings like *The Sower* and *The Gleaners* (above) have a haunting quality with their flat, melancholy landscape, drab colors, and isolated figures.

Impressionism

The Impressionists were the most important breakaway group of artists to emerge during the nineteenth century. They included Claude Monet (1840-1926), Pierre Auguste Renoir (1841-1919), Camille Pissarro (1830-1903), and Alfred Sisley (1839-1899). They rejected classical and historical themes and chose modern subjects like people boating on the Seine River or relaxing in Parisian cafés and parks or at the theater or ballet. They wanted to capture the immediate visual impression of what they saw under changing conditions of light and weather. They painted landscapes in the open air, working in bright sunlight, and they experimented with techniques, using short strokes or dots of color and avoiding dark outlines and traditional ways of painting light and shade. Critics thought their paintings looked sketchy and unfinished, and their works were rejected by the official Paris Salon. From 1874, the Impressionists held their own exhibitions in Paris, becoming the most important and influential art movement in the second half of the nineteenth century. The Impressionists and the Post-Impressionists who followed them, including such famous nineteenth-century artists as Paul Cézanne (1839-1906) and Vincent van Gogh (1853-90), are discussed separately in *Impressionism*, another book in this series. Above is a view of Paris, *Place de Havre*, by Camille Pissarro. *Chicago Art Institute.*

8 JAPANESE ART

The Carpenter's Yard by Katsushika Hokusai, one of the celebrated Ukiyo-e artists of nineteenth-century Japan. This is one of his *Thirty-six Views of Mount Fuji. British Museum, London.*

Japanese artists had become skilled at color printing from woodblocks during the eighteenth century: up to thirty blocks (one for each color) were used to print a single design. The Ukiyo-e, or "Floating World," school specialized in scenes of everyday life, at home or in town, and portraits of actors and actresses. These decorative prints were pasted to walls or screens in the home and used to illustrate books and greetings cards. Landscapes and bird and flower prints were also popular.

European artists first saw Japanese prints in the nineteenth century, when some arrived in Paris as packing for china. Artists, including the Impressionists, were impressed by the Japanese printmakers' strong sense of design and pattern, unusual compositions and bold, flat areas of color.

The decorative appeal and inventiveness of Japanese prints is illustrated by the *Thirty-six Views of Mount Fuji* by Katsushika Hokusai (1760-1849). Hokusai had begun making

The Revenge of Igagoe by Uragawa Kuniyoshi, another Ukiyo-e artist. Kuniyoshi often illustrated the Samurai warriors of Japanese history. In this print he has shown a warrior engaged in fighting off his foes in a style similar to one used in modern Western cartoon comics.

theatrical prints in the Ukiyo-e style but soon became more interested in landscape. As well as his series focusing on the dramatic, cone-shaped mountain near Tokyo, he printed series of *Waterfalls*, *Bridges*, and *Flowers*. His strong, stylized designs and brilliant colors were admired by Edouard Manet and the Impressionists.

Ando Hiroshige (1797-1858) trained in the Ukiyo-e school, but from the 1830s he concentrated on bird and flower themes and landscapes. He is most admired for his sensitive treatment of light, weather, and atmosphere in landscapes in mist, rain, or snow.

Uragawa Kuniyoshi (1798-1861) took his subjects from Japanese history and legend. His large, often humorous color prints, sometimes showing samurai warriors engaged in violent battles with monsters, are as bold and melodramatic in style as the illustrations in Western comic books.

9 PRINTMAKING AND PHOTOGRAPHY

The English artist and poet William Blake (1757-1827) made this print to illustrate the Book of Job. The print was produced from a colored engraving.

During the nineteenth century, wood engraving, a method of printmaking that uses blocks of hard wood, allowed faster and cheaper reproduction for book and magazine illustration and copies of popular paintings. Wood engraving involved the use of very hard wooden blocks for printing. The wood was cut across the grain (from sections across the trunk of a tree) rather than parallel to the tree (along the trunk) as in the older art of woodcut. Wood engraving allows clean fine lines to be cut into the block. Those lines show as white in the print because ink was only rolled onto the uncut section.

Woodcut had been widely used in the fifteenth century. It enjoyed a revival from the 1830s with the increasing interest in medieval art. Later in the century it was used by Arts and Crafts artists to illustrate books of legend, poetry, and history (see pages 42, 43, and 44).

Lithography, a new method of surface printing from stone, was invented at the end of the

Above Honoré Daumier's cartoons poked fun at the pretensions of middle class life. The lithograph shows a couple in front of their portrait at a Paris salon.

Right *The Guardian Angel*, a photograph taken in 1868 by English photographer Julia Margaret Cameron (1815-1879). She created haunting images, often with religious or literary themes.

eighteenth century. The artist's design was drawn on the lithographic stone in greasy crayon or ink and fixed with chemicals. The stone surface was then wetted with water and covered with ink that stuck only to the greasy parts of the design. The stone was then passed through a press to transfer the inked design onto paper.

As well as being cheap, lithography could be used for simple linear designs and color prints and could make huge numbers of copies.

Various effects with opaque or delicate textured washes could be achieved. In France, it became the popular medium for magazine cartoons and caricatures, such as those by the political and social satirist Honoré Daumier (1808-1879).

By the end of the century, color lithography was being used for a new art form: the poster. The French artist Henri de Toulouse-Lautrec (1864-1901) began designing posters in 1891. His subjects were dancers and circus clowns

Woman Washing, a print by the American artist Mary Cassatt (see page 43). Her work was greatly influenced by the art of Japanese woodblock printers, whose work she saw when she was living in Paris.

and scenes from music halls, theaters, café bars, and Paris night clubs, like the Moulin Rouge cabaret. Lautrec was inspired by Japanese woodblock prints, choosing unusual viewpoints, flattening space, and using bold colors and semi-abstract shapes to design lively, colorful images.

Photography was the technique that had the greatest impact on nineteenth century art. The amateur inventor Joseph-Nicéphore Niepce had discovered in the 1820s how to fix negatives to a metal plate using bitumen. Another Frenchman, Louis Daguerre, was using a silvered copper plate to make "daguerreotype" prints by the 1830s. The first true photographs – negatives from which any number of prints could be taken – were made by the English scientist William Henry Fox Talbot around 1840. He discovered how to make negatives by soaking paper in silver chloride to make it light sensitive, then exposing it to light through a lens.

Modern poster art began with the lively color lithographs of Henri de Toulouse-Lautrec. He was a superb draftsman with a wonderful gift for conveying movement and atmosphere in a few simple strokes.

Mezzotint was a popular method for reproducing artists' works. The engraver roughened a copper or steel plate with a tool to produce a burr (an overall textured surface), which could catch the ink and print velvety black. Designs and lighter areas could then be produced by reducing or removing the textured burr by scraping or polishing the surface of the plate. Mezzotints spread the fame of artists by allowing people to buy cheap printed copies of their works.

Aquatint, a method of etching in soft tones, was especially suitable for reproducing the soft and transparent effects of watercolors and wash drawings. Powdered resin was shaken onto a copper plate and fixed to it by heating. Some areas were then removed to print darker while others were blocked out with varnish to print lighter, and then the plate was dipped in acid, which produced a pitted or textured surface, producing the grainy effect of watercolor when printed.

10 THE END OF THE CENTURY

Right "Woodpecker" tapestry, designed by William Morris c.1885. *William Morris Gallery, London.*

Far right *Isolde*, a magazine illustration by the English artist Aubrey Beardsley (1872-1898). His stylized drawings are typical of the Art Nouveau style of the 1890s. *Private collection.*

ISOLDE

The invention of labor-saving machines and mass-production of goods and materials in factories and workshops altered people's lifestyles and their clothes, furniture, and household goods. Although machines generally improved the quality of people's lives, they led to a decline in manufacturing standards, which by the end of the century was becoming increasingly apparent. In England, a growing awareness of the need to preserve qualities of design and craftsmanship inspired the founding of the Arts and Crafts movement, led by the artist-designer William Morris (1834-1896) and the influential art critic John Ruskin (1819-1900).

The Arts and Crafts movement rejected the shoddy standards of mass production and the fussy and over-elaborate designs that had become popular. Arts and Crafts designers took inspiration from the art of the Middle Ages, establishing an "Art-workers Guild" that was based on medieval artists' guilds and drew on Gothic motifs and style.

In 1861 Morris founded the firm of Morris, Marshall Faulkner & Co., with workshops producing handmade furniture, stained glass, carpets, tapestries, wallpapers, and fabrics to designs by Morris and artists including Dante Gabriel Rossetti and Edward Coley Burne-

Women artists in the nineteenth century

In nineteenth-century Europe and America, sketching and watercolor painting were popular pastimes for women of the middle and upper classes. Working as a professional artist, however, was not generally considered a suitable occupation, although some did succeed in exhibiting and selling their work. In England, Helen Allingham (1849-1926) painted charming cottage and garden scenes in watercolors with painstaking detail, and Kate Greenaway (1846-1901) used watercolors for her delicate illustrations for children's books. In France, Rosa Bonheur (1822-1899) specialized in painting animals, especially horses, exhibiting regularly at the Paris Salon after 1841. Mary Cassatt (1845-1926), an American working in Paris, and Berthe Morisot (1841-1895) were both Impressionist artists. Cassatt painted women and children in soft oils or pastels and produced prints strongly influenced by the Japanese style (see page 40). Early on, Morisot was influenced by the French painter Corot, but after marrying Edouard Manet's younger brother, she joined the Impressionists. She painted interiors and garden scenes with fresh, flickering brush strokes. Women also played an important part in the Arts and Crafts movement, as painters, illustrators, potters, metalworkers, and embroiderers. *A Waggon and a Team of Horses* (above) is by Rosa Bonheur. *Wallace Collection, London.*

Jones (1833-1898). Morris's distinctive designs with their closely worked decorative patterns became very popular and are still being printed and sold today. When he married, Morris asked his friend, architect Philip Webb (1831-1915) to design a house for him. The Red House in Kent, England, took its inspiration from traditional English manor houses and the Gothic Revival style and encouraged a new style in architecture.

Exhibitions of Arts and Crafts work and design magazines like *The Studio* spread the influence of this new style. Soon every branch of the arts was affected, including book design and illustration, with the founding of Morris's own Kelmscott Press in 1890.

In the United States, the Arts and Crafts style inspired the setting up of art potteries like the Rookwood Pottery in Cincinnati in 1880, which

Above An earthenware dish painted with a peacock pattern, designed by William Frend De Morgan (1839-1917). He illustrated pottery and ceramics in designs taken from Turkish and Persian art.

Right A Rookwood Pottery earthenware jar made in the United States around the turn of the century.

produced decorative vases and jugs with rich green or brown glazes, and the Newcomb College Pottery in 1895. In New York, Elbert Hubbard (1856-1915) founded a Guild of Craftsmen, the Roycrofters, based on Morris's ideas. They made oak furniture, metalwork, and books. Another furniture designer, Gustav Stickley (1858-1942), designed furniture influenced by the Arts and Crafts pieces he had seen on a visit to Europe.

By the end of the century, new attitudes toward painting were emerging under the influence of photography and the Impressionist movement. Some artists, reacting against storytelling genre pictures and detailed, photographic-type paintings, began to experiment with imaginative subjects and freer brushwork. The American painter James Whistler, who settled in London in 1859, believed that painting should affect people in the same way as music. He used free, soft brush strokes, concentrating on tone, color, and pattern rather than line. As a student in Paris, Whistler had studied the works of the Spanish master Velázquez in the Louvre,

THE LATER CENTURY 45

Charles Rennie Mackintosh (1868-1928)

Mackintosh was a Scottish architect and designer prominent in the Arts and Crafts movement. He achieved great success, particularly in Europe where his elegant designs were greatly admired. His design for the Glasgow School of Art (begun in 1896) is considered to be the first original example of Art Nouveau architecture in Great Britain, although much of his work, including his graceful furnishings and interior decor, are quite unlike Art Nouveau. This beautifully proportioned room at the School of Art (above), with its tall bay windows and granite fireplace, houses some of Mackintosh's larger pieces of furniture.

Whistler's *Nocturne in Black and Gold: The Falling Rocket*. The painting triggered a famous libel case between the artist and the critic John Ruskin. *Institute of Arts, Detroit.*

admiring their cool gray tones and uncluttered sense of form and pattern. He also admired living French painters like Courbet and was impressed by the Japanese prints then becoming popular in Europe.

In his own works, whether portraits, interiors, or scenes on the Thames River, Whistler tended to simplify and flatten space, concentrating on shape and pattern and often using cool colors. He used musical terms such as symphony, arrangement, and nocturne to name many of his paintings. *Nocturne in Black and Gold: The Falling Rocket*, painted in 1875, was inspired by a display of fireworks over a London park. Its free, semi-abstract design shocked the critics and led to a famous libel trial in which Whistler sued the art critic John Ruskin for accusing him of "flinging a pot of paint in the public's face." During the 1860s, Whistler began signing his works with a butterfly motif, which reflected the decorative charm of his works (see also picture on page 9). With their simplified forms and cool, clear tones, Whistler's paintings heralded the art of the coming twentieth century.

GLOSSARY

Abstract art Images based on shapes and forms, not representing anything else.

Allegorical An image or theme used to symbolize something else.

Anatomy The science concerned with the physical structure of animals and plants.

Art Nouveau A style of art and architecture in the 1890s. It was characterized by flowing, coiling outlines and stylized natural forms such as flowers and leaves.

Barbizon School A group of landscape painters based at the village of Barbizon in the Forest of Fontainebleau in France in the mid-nineteenth century.

Biblical Relating to the Bible.

Bronze A type of metal, made from copper and tin, used for making tools and sculpture.

Ceramics The art of producing objects in clay, porcelain, china, etc.

Classical mythology Stories and beliefs relating to ancient Greece and Rome.

Derby Day The day of the famous annual horse race, held at Epsom Downs in Surrey, England, every June.

Engraving A print made from an engraved (cut) hard surface such as metal, wood, or stone.

Etching A method of printmaking using acid to burn a design onto metal or glass.

Form Shape.

Fresco A way of painting directly onto newly plastered walls. The picture itself is often called a fresco.

Genre Artwork that shows people doing everyday activities.

Gothic The style of architecture first used in western Europe from the twelfth to sixteenth centuries.

Gothic Revival A style in the nineteenth century that imitated medieval Gothic.

Hudson River School A group of American artists centered in or near the Hudson River Valley in the 1800s.

Impressionism The name given to the art of a group of painters working in the latter half of the nineteenth century who concentrated on recording the effects of light and color.

Idealized Represented in an ideal or perfect form rather than naturally.

Industrial Revolution The time during the eighteenth and nineteenth centuries when European countries and the United States changed from producing mainly agricultural goods to mainly industrial goods.

Interiors Pictures of the inside of rooms or buildings.

Lithography A method of making prints from a lithographic stone on which a design is made with a greasy crayon or ink and then pressed onto paper.

Media In art, the different materials and methods of production.

Middle Ages The period between the end of the Dark Ages (at the end of the Roman Empire) to the Renaissance, from about the sixth to sixteenth centuries.

Moral Concerned with a sense of right and wrong.

Nazarenes A group of artists working in Germany in the early nineteenth century.

Neoclassical A late eighteenth- and early nineteenth-century style of art and architecture based on the imitation of surviving ancient Greek and Roman models.

Panoramas Wide landscape views in all directions.

Patronage The support given by a person (patron) who sponsors or aids artists.

Perspective The science of showing objects in space on a two-dimensional (flat) surface.

Pre-Raphaelites A group of artists in nineteenth-century England who painted in the detailed style they considered to be typical of medieval and early Renaissance artists.

Realism A style of art that seeks to represent familiar, everyday aspects of life.

Resin A plant substance used for hardening.

Romanticism A movement in the arts in the late eighteenth and nineteenth centuries characterized by an emphasis on emotions and feeling.

Royal Academy A society founded in London in 1768 to encourage painting, sculpture, and design in England.

Samurai warriors Japanese fighters and aristocrats.

Symbolism The representation of something by something else.

Tempera Painting with pigments (colors) mixed with egg yolks and water. This was a common painting technique until the late fifteenth century.

Tone The quality of color.

Visionary A spiritual person who has visions of another life.

Woodcuts Prints made by cutting areas of a block of wood to form a picture. When the block is covered with ink and pressed on paper, the cut design is printed.

FURTHER READING

American Heritage Illustrated History of of the United States, Vol. 8: The Civil War. Reprint of 1964 edition. Westbury, NY: Choice Pub NY, 1988.

Beneduce, Ann K. *A Weekend with Winslow Homer.* New York: Rizzoli International, 1993.

Berman, Avis. *James McNeill Whistler.* New York: Harry N. Abrams Inc., 1993.

Cain, Michael. *Mary Cassatt: Artist.* American Women of Achievement. New York: Chelsea House, 1989.

Janson, H. W. and Janson, Anthony F. *The History of Art for Young People.* 4th edition. New York: Harry N. Abrams Inc., 1992.

Kastner, Joseph. *John James Audubon.* New York: Harry N. Abrams Inc., 1992.

McHugh, Christopher. *Western Art 1600-1800.* Art and Artists. Thomson Learning, 1994.

Roalf, Peggy. *Landscapes.* Looking at Paintings. New York: Hyperion, 1992.

Sullivan, George. *Mathew Brady: His Life and Photographs.* New York: Dutton Children's Books, 1994.

WHERE TO SEE NINETEENTH-CENTURY ART

The following list of museums includes some of the most important American museums for viewing art of the nineteenth century.

Baltimore
The Baltimore Museum of Art
Art Museum Drive
Baltimore, MD 21218
(301) 396-7101

Boston
Museum of Fine Arts
465 Huntington Avenue
Boston, MA 02115
(617) 267-9300

Chicago
The Art Institute of Chicago
Michigan Avenue at Adams Street
Chicago, IL 60603
(312) 443-3600

Cincinnati
Cincinnati Art Museum
Eden Park
Cincinnati, OH 45202
(513) 721-5204

Cleveland
Cleveland Museum of Art
11150 East Boulevard
Cleveland, OH 44106
(216) 421-7340

Houston
The Museum of Fine Arts
1001 Bissonet
Box 6826
Houston, TX 77265
(713) 639-7300

Los Angeles
Los Angeles County Museum of Art
5905 Wilshire Boulevard
Los Angeles, CA 90036
(213) 857-6111

New Britain
The New Britain Museum of
  American Art
56 Lexington Street
New Britain, CT 06052
(203) 229-0257

New York
The Metropolitan Museum of Art
Fifth Avenue at 82nd Street
New York, NY 10028
(212) 879-5500

Philadelphia
Philadelphia Museum of Art
26th Street and Benjamin
  Franklin Parkway
Philadelphia, PA 19101
(215) 763-8100

San Francisco
The Fine Arts Museums of California
M. H. deYoung Museum
Lincoln Park
San Francisco, CA 94121
(415) 750-3600

Washington D.C.
The National Museum of
  American Art
Smithsonian Institution
8th and G Streets, NW
Washington, DC 20560
(202) 357-2700

INDEX